MEN ARE PIGS

(IT'S OUR BIRTHRIGHT!)

The truth, the whole truth, and nothing but the politically incorrect truth.

DAVID SPRINGMEYER

GENERAL PUBLISHING GROUP
Los Angeles

Publisher: W. Quay Hays
Editor: Colby Allerton
Art Director: Susan Anson

For Information:
General Publishing Group, Inc.
2701 Ocean Park Boulevard
Santa Monica, California 90405

Library of Congress Catalog Card Number: 96-080299
ISBN: 1-57544-022-9

Printed in the USA
10 9 8 7 6 5 4 3 2 1

General Publishing Group
Los Angeles

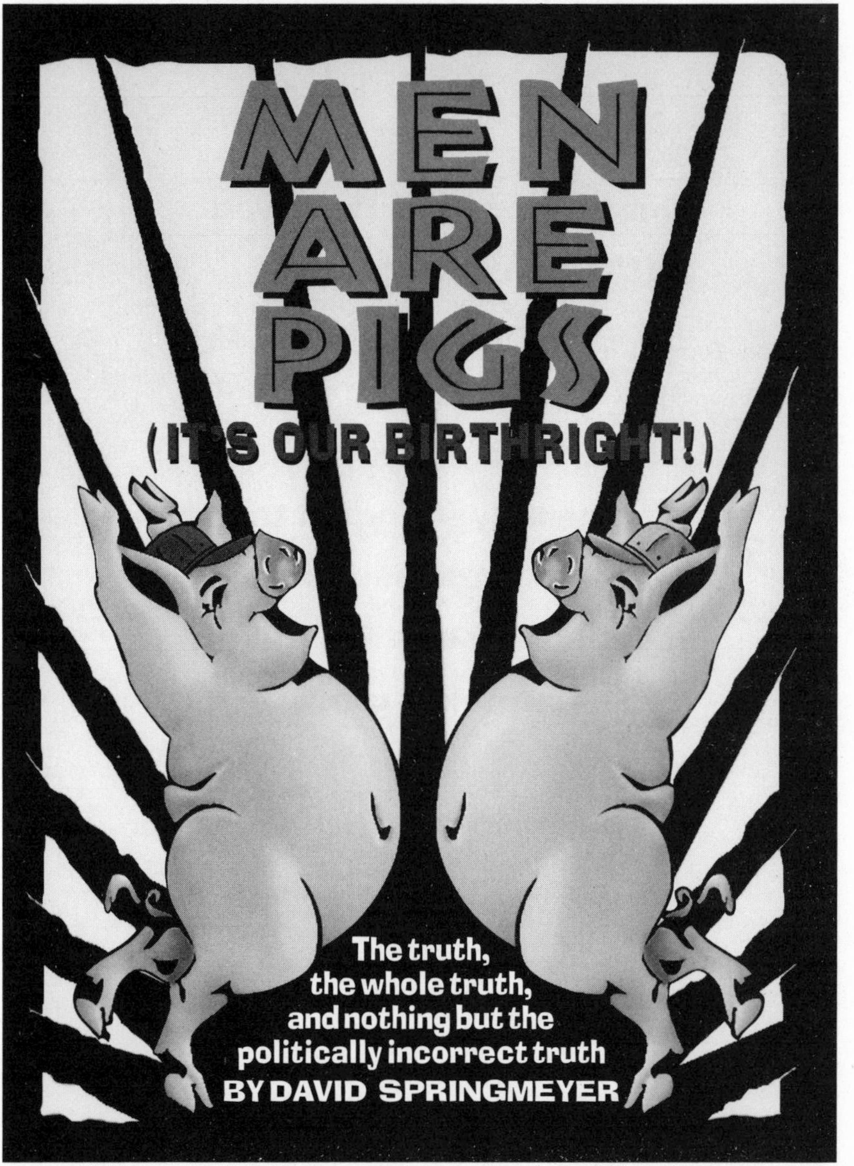
MEN ARE PIGS
(IT'S OUR BIRTHRIGHT!)
The truth,
the whole truth,
and nothing but the
politically incorrect truth
BY DAVID SPRINGMEYER

One day a man will take you
on the high roads;
After a time he'll leave you
someplace nice or tell you
where the big boys play.
They usually string out their
games in someone's shadow.
It could be yours. More likely
mine, for mine's grown longer
and there's more room here.

Rod McKuen

INTRODUCTION

This brave new world sucks. I find myself, along with those of my gender, caught up in a struggle to maintain a paradigm that our culture would have us believe has outlived its usefulness, being a man. Until recently, being a man was a fairly simple task, a task which most men embraced with joy, if not total dignity. Things have changed. Men are now expected to be something more than just men; they are expected to embrace their feminine side, and in doing so, to reject aspects of their being that conflict with what is fast becoming a society dominated by a code of standards established and enforced by women. We find that areas once roamed freely by men are fast disappearing from our culture, the result of a restructuring of society that has gone just a bit too far to suit the male of the species.

In the good old days, before the sexual revolution, men knew things, big things, deep things, things that helped a man define the boundaries of his world. There was a time when that knowledge brought a man a measure of respect in the community and, depending on how much he knew and how willing he was to share that knowledge, status within the male sub-culture.

One of the responsibilities of being a man, a keeper of that knowledge, was the obligation to share that knowledge with other men. This sharing of the paradigm began at a very young age, father to son, brother to brother. As men grew, the task of knowledge transfer fell upon the shoulders of their peers and usually took place in locker rooms, bars and frat houses. Somewhere, between the sexual revolution and the Equal Rights Amendment, we lost contact with all that was good about being a man. We stopped sharing the knowledge, fearing that women wouldn't see us as sensitive men, worthy of their attention and favors.

We are in danger of losing our grip on our manhood, so to speak. We, and our culture, are allowing our sons to be taught how to be men, not by other men in dens of iniquity, smoking cheap cigars, but by a purple dragon who spends his day dancing, singing insipid songs and playing games that don't involve a bat or a ball.

The time has come to begin sharing that knowledge again, before it's too late. Our sons must know the truth. That men are special because they are different. That men know things that set them apart from women. As you read this book you will smile and you will laugh. You will find yourself saying things like "I knew that," as though you were discovering yourself again.

This book is also for women, for its pages contain all that any woman would want to know about the man in her life. Here you will find all that is good and noble about him. You'll be charmed by his wit and humor, his unique way of looking at life. Here too is the dark side, the qualities that your mother warned you about, but you can't resist. After reading this book, you will understand men as you never dreamed possible.

This book contains some of what men know. This knowledge has been shared with me by many men, over the course of many years. Pass it on.

Men Are Pigs!

Men know they are pigs; it's their birthright.

Men know that there are two kinds of men: pigs and scum-sucking pigs. It is a father's duty to spend an excessive amount of energy steering their daughters away from the scum-sucking type.

Men know that their jock strap is their friend and that a cup is their best friend.

Men know never to kiss an ugly woman, the memory can never be erased.

Men know that you should win if you can, lose if you must, but cheat.

Men know that men are from here and women are from way the hell over there.

Men know that when in doubt, don't whip it out.

Men know never to accept a blind date.

Men know that using a condom is like kissing your sister, but it's better than paying child support to a woman you wouldn't bring to church on Easter Sunday.

Men know never to bend over in the locker room shower to pick up a bar of soap. It pays to buy a soap-on-a-rope.

Men know not to play pool with someone who owns their own pearl-handled cue.

Men know that the good die young.

Men know that the first rule of life is to party till you puke.

Men know that more than a mouthful is wasted.

Men know that shit happens.

Men know that it's not how, it's how many.

Men know that they get married to have sex
and women have sex to get married.

Men know that a car is just a motel room
on wheels.

Men know that women have legs so that they
can leave when you're finished with them.

Men know that nice guys finish last.

Men know that you should never date your
sister's college roommate.

Men know that you should avoid the opera
unless you speak Italian and like to listen to
fat women sing.

Men know that it's not over until the fat lady sings.

Men know to always check your fly before leaving the men's room.

Men know that once is never enough. Unless you're referring to seeing your grandmother naked.

Men know that real men don't go to the ballet.

Men know that when showering with your teammates, always maintain eye contact.

Men know that it's never a good idea to tell your father-in-law how good his daughter is in bed.

Men know that if your buddies are helping you move, never offer them a beer until the job is completed.

Men know that eventually a woman will say yes.

Men know that they should never admit to being a virgin to their buddies.

Men know that eventually a woman will end up looking like her mother.

Men know that there is no such thing as a sure thing, unless her name is Bambi.

Men know that you never really know someone until you've seen them naked.

Men know that if a woman slips her tongue in your mouth, it's a sure sign that she's the friendly sort.

Men know never to marry a woman from West Virginia without first checking for webbed toes.

Men know that if a man asks you to dance, you're in the wrong bar.

Men know that no one lives forever and you'll never get what you want. Keeping that in mind, everything else is a gift.

Men know never to room with a guy whose nickname is stinky.

Men know that no matter where you hide your *Playboys*, your mother will find them.

Men know that once you tell a woman that you love her, you can never take it back without a nasty scene.

Men know that if someone tells you you're full of shit, it's more than likely the truth.

Men know that you should never try to picture your parents making love. (Got ya!)

Men know never to use a condom purchased from a machine in the men's room of a country western bar.

Men know never to use a condom if you can't remember when and where you purchased the thing.

Men know that if you can't remember the last time you had sex, it's been too long and there's probably no hope for you.

Men know that you should never date a woman who carries a twelve pack of glow in the dark condoms in her purse.

Men know that it's not a good idea to list *Deep Throat* as one of your favorite movies on a dating service questionnaire.

Men know never to use a glow-in-the-dark condom on the first date. You can scare the hell out of someone with one of those things.

Men know that men and women want the same thing, men just want it sooner and more often.

Men know that you should attend a college at least 750 miles away. Any closer and it's too easy for your parents or your girlfriend to show up unannounced.

Men know that if you're planning to break up with a woman, do it before her birthday or Christmas. No need spending good money on a lost cause.

Men know that it's a lot easier to make a woman cry than it is to make her laugh.

Men know that a woman will never love you as much as she loves her father and her children.

Men know that women expect them to be intuitive, an assumption that has ruined many an otherwise good relationship.

Men know that they don't have a clue when it comes to women.

Men know that easy jobs don't pay much.

Men know that if it were easy, everyone would be doing it.

Men know that it's not just a game.

Men know that the higher someone climbs up the tree, the easier it is to shoot him in the ass.

Men know that if you stick your nose in someone's business, they're likely to stick their business in your nose.

Men know never to admit anything, especially to your wife.

Men know that an extra large jock strap has nothing to do with the size of your tool.

Men know that just because a shirt is five years old is not a reason for throwing it away.

Men know that no one needs more than six pairs of shoes at any one time during their life.

Men know that they get mad, women get even.

Men know that women want to marry someone like their father and that men want to marry someone like Christy Brinkley.

Men know that no one remembers who came
in second.

Men know that winning is everything.

Men know that they do grow up, they just
remember how much fun it was to be young.

Men know that it's never a good idea to keep
letters from past loves.

Men know to tell it like it is. Women tell it like
they'd like it to be.

Men know that it's not a good idea to stick a wad
of chewing tobacco in your mouth just
before playing a game of tongue tag with
your girlfriend.

Men know that no matter how long they live,
they're never going to get enough sex.

Men know how to forgive and forget. Women forgive but never forget.

Men know that they always forget to put the seat down. They also know that women never put the seat up.

Men know that it's just easier to squeeze from the top.

Men know how to play by the rules. Women make up the rules as they go along.

Men know how to take someone at their word. Women want collateral.

Men know how to put women on a pedestal. Women know how to put men on the defensive.

Men know that it's a good idea to go home for a nooner every once in a while.

Men know that in a fight you should kick the other guy in the balls at the first opportunity.

Men know better than to eat anything they've never seen before.

Men know that the reason people don't like cats is because they don't know how to cook them.

Men know better than to eat at a restaurant that advertises "Good Food."

Men know better than to begin negotiation until they have the upper hand.

Men know not to tell their lawyer everything.

Men know never to throw up in their father-in-law's car.

Sometimes a cigar is just a cigar.

Sigmund Freud

Men know to dance with big-breasted women whenever the opportunity avails itself.

Men know what women want; we're just not going to give it to them without one damn good fight.

Men know that the man and the boy can coexist.

Men know when their careers have peaked.

Men know how to make a woman happy, at least before marriage.

Men know how to lie.

Men know how to tell the truth.

Men know that truth is a matter of black and white, right and wrong.

Men know that telling little white lies is OK in order to keep someone from being hurt.

Men know that you can't love two women at the same time.

Men know when not to call a woman.

Men know when they should call a woman but often choose not to do so for reasons not totally clear to them.

Men know that a woman wants to say yes, she's just looking for the right reason.

Men know all of the right reasons why a woman should say yes.

Men know that another man is gay. At least they like to think that they know.

Men know how to find their way without a map.
We've been doing it for millions of years.

Men know how to spit without having it run
down their chin and onto their shirt.

Men know not to piss into the wind.

Men know that when it comes to being on time,
women aren't.

Men know that the road belongs to them.

Men know that God invented the remote control
as a gift for men.

Men know that God is a man, not a woman.

Men know when their wives or girlfriends find
another man attractive.

Men know which is the salad fork and which is not, they just don't give a rat's ass.

Men know how far they can go.

Men know that it's more fun to hang around with the guys than it is to spend quality time with a woman.

Men know that no matter how much they love a woman, their jobs will always be more important to them, and more interesting.

Men know that they are defined by their work and how much money they make.

Men know that all the important things they have learned were learned in the locker room and on the playing field.

Men know how to mend fences.

Men know when to keep their mouths shut.

Men know when to bite their tongues.

Men know how important it is to be able to walk with the big dogs.

Men know how to keep a woman interested.

Men know just what to do in order to get a woman to dump them.

Men know that in an emergency they can be counted on to help.

Men know that there are more than two ways to skin a cat and to blow your nose.

Men know that women cannot be trusted.

Men know never to confuse their wife's motives with their mother's instincts.

Men know how dangerous it is to compare their wife's cooking with that of their mother.

Men know how to tell a dirty joke. Women like to pretend that they don't like a good dirty joke.

Men know that women are not as interested about a man's body as a man is about a woman's body.

Men know that a naked woman is ten times more dangerous than one who is fully clothed.

Men know that their ex-wife is a piece of luggage they'll have to carry forever.

Men know how easy it is to fall in love.

Men know how hard it is to keep loving the
same woman.

Men know the price that must be paid for being
caught looking at another woman.

Men know every anniversary and birthday;
they're just not as important as last
weekend's big game.

Men know that they live their lives alone.

Men know that they can never measure up to
their wife's father.

Men know that women don't trust them.

Men know what makes children happy.

Men know that they do not have an inherited need to change their underwear every day.

Men know, deep down in their heart and soul, that they are every bit as good as they were when they were twenty-five, they just can't prove it.

Men know that it's impossible to make a woman happy for more than an hour.

Men know who they can trust.

Men know who will trust them.

Men know that the first time they had sex was just as exciting as the first time they masturbated.

Men know that form is everything.

Men know that it's important to keep score.

Men know that letting your son play with dolls after his fourth birthday is a violation of one of the basic rules of life.

Men know when a woman is beginning to think about marriage.

Men know how to jump-start a car.

Men know how to jump-start a woman.

Men know that women don't have much respect for men.

Men know that a woman will wear a low-cut dress and expect them to stare at her cleavage. Men also know that the woman will get ticked off when they do, for reasons not totally clear to them.

Men know that there is nothing sexier than a woman on the make.

Men know that a woman will order the most expensive item on the menu and wait to see their reaction.

Men know that women are constantly testing our commitment.

Men know that women expect men to act like jerks.

Men know who their real friends are.

Men know how to keep a secret.

Men know not to bring a knife to a gunfight.

Men know when to give in.

Men know when to give up.

Men know that foods that taste good are bad for you and foods that taste bad are good for you.

Men know that eventually someone will put the cap back on the toothpaste.

Men know that with a little ingenuity, two wrongs can make a right.

Men know that proctologists don't enjoy it any more than they do.

Men know that lawyers are lower than whale shit.

Men know that you don't need to know how to spell as long as you have a good spell checker.

Men know that most women know how to swear like a truck driver.

Men are nicotine-soaked, beer-besmerched, whiskey-greased, red-eyed devils.

Carry Nation

Men know that wet wood won't burn.

Men know that VCRs, quantum physics and
women are beyond the understanding of
mortal men.

Men know that one road is as good as the next.

Men know that neatness counts, but not
for much.

Men know that no one will ever love them as
much as their daughters.

Men know that fat men don't look good in three-
piece suits and Speedos.

Men know that home improvement contractors
were lawyers in a previous life.

Men know that suicide is sometimes a
viable option.

Men know that hot cars are babe magnets.

Men know not to lend money to their
brother-in-law.

Men know that life isn't fair; it should be,
but it's not.

Men know that there's no such thing as an
honest lawyer.

Men know that if the dog hadn't stopped to take
a shit, he would have caught the rabbit.

Men know that no man can live up to his
wife's expectations.

Men know never to give their wife an electrical
appliance as an anniversary gift.

Men know that it's dangerous to fart in an empty elevator. You never know who's going to get on at the next stop.

Men know that calling your mother will only encourage her.

Men know that it's easier to impress a woman's mother than her father.

Men know that when a woman tells you that you're not meeting her needs, it won't be long before she tells you not to let the door hit your ass on the way out.

Men know that from time to time, it is absolutely necessary to adjust oneself.

Men know that eventually all jobs suck.

Men know when it's time to stop.

Men know that there's nothing more relaxing than a healthy shit or a good screw.

Men know better than to keep a woman waiting.

Men know how dangerous a divorced woman can be.

Men know what type of men to advise their daughters to stay away from.

Men know to keep their cash in a money clip in a front pocket of their pants.

Men know that the aisle seat on a plane provides the most room and comfort.

Men know that singing in the shower is good therapy.

Men know how to build things.

Men know that they don't need to read the instructions.

Men know no shame.

Men know what the score is.

Men know that they are not as dumb as they look.

Men know that they're not quite as stupid as people think.

Men know that there is nothing quite as painful as being kicked in the balls.

Men know that it's possible to go blind by looking at a fat woman in a bikini.

Men know that no one has ever gone blind doing it.

Men know that balancing a checkbook is something that a woman does better than a man.

Men know not to expect sex after marriage to be as good as sex before marriage, or as often.

Men know never to question their wife about how many pairs of shoes she owns.

Men know that no matter what your wife is wearing, the correct comment is "You look good in that outfit!"

Men know exactly why their wives love to watch the soaps.

Men know to shower and shave before sex.

Men know that a woman would like them to smell good.

Men know how to fight dirty.

Men know how to cheat and not get caught.

Men know when it's that time of the month.

Men know when it's getting close to that time
of the month.

Men know the rules to most of the games.

Men know that you can cheat an honest man.
It's pretty damn easy.

Men know that every woman believes that she
can change a man.

Men know that there's no way that any woman
is going to change him unless he wants
to change.

Men know that if you run out of clean socks, it's OK to look in the clothes hamper for a pair.

Men know exactly how much gas is left in the tank and how far that gas will get them.

Men know that there is a small degree of satisfaction to be derived from doing battle with some of life's windmills.

Men know that you can't fight city hall.

Men know that when the shit hits the fan, it's time to duck.

Men know that at some point in their career they will be discriminated against because of their gender.

Men know that everyone has a glass ceiling.

Men know that you can teach a dog new
tricks. It just takes a lot longer and requires
the patience of Job and the craft of Skinner.

Men know that a woman would rather shop
than have sex.

Men know that women may want to
communicate, but that doesn't mean that
they want to listen to what you have to say.

Men know when to draw a line in the sand.

Men know how to repair things.

Men know how to destroy things.

Men know how to drive fast.

Men know when they're getting a good haircut and when they're being scalped.

Men know when the service has been good or bad and how much to leave as a tip.

Men know when a woman wants to leave.

Men know if a woman wants to stay.

Men know how to give back rubs.

Men know when a woman is more interested in his salary than him.

Men know how to daydream.

The main difference between men and women is that men are lunatics and women are idiots.

Rebecca West

Men know what to say in order to make a
woman mad.

Men know how to drive a woman crazy in the
first year of marriage.

Men know that the only correct answer to a
question about a woman's new hairstyle is
"It is very attractive." Any other answer
invites at least two hours of backtracking.

Men know if a woman's friends like him or not.

Men know when their children are lying to them.

Men know when their children are troubled.

Men know that there are many enjoyable ways
to get even.

Men know when to take seconds and when
to pass.

Men know that a best friend is something everyone needs.

Men know that in order to avoid grief and make their wife happy, they will have to attend church on a regular basis.

Men know that women want a man who can dance.

Men know that giving flowers to a woman for no apparent reason is a sure way to gain points.

Men know where to look for the easy way out.

Men know how to use firearms.

Men know who to lie to and who to avoid lying to.

Men know that a woman can be their best friend or their worst enemy.

Men know on which side their bread is buttered.

Men know an ugly woman when they see one.

Men know that they prefer large breasts on a woman (as opposed to a man).

Men know that most of us have a thing about blondes.

Men know when they need a haircut but will wait another two weeks before getting one.

Men know that propping your feet up on the kitchen table to cut your toenails is not a good idea.

Men know that boogers are not God's answer to the worldwide famine problem.

Men know that only a good friend will tell you that you have something green and slimy hanging from your nose.

Men know that a fart will burn when a match is held close to the escaping gas. Not something to be tried by the faint of heart.

Men know how to write in the snow with their piss. That's why you tell your children never to eat yellow snow.

Men know which side of the bed to sleep on for the greatest amount of comfort.

Men know that someone who farts in the bathtub for amusement is known as a dork.

Men know that for every action movie their wife agrees to see, they will have to sit through at least five chick movies.

Men know that a woman will tell you she doesn't want popcorn at the movie and proceed to eat most of yours.

Men know that a woman will tell another woman things that she won't tell her therapist.

Men know not to buy a woman clothing as a gift. It will only be returned for something that she will refer to as suitable.

Men know that spending an hour in a hardware store is better for your mental health than spending the same amount of time with a therapist.

Men know that the only way to make a hardware store better is to install a lunch counter.

Men know that if God meant men to change diapers he would have made what comes out of a body smell like Aqua Velva.

Men know that they would rather shovel out the stalls in a dairy barn than change a diaper.

Men know that only the TV remote control is more important than the sports page.

Men know that women don't get *The Far Side*.

Men know every good hot-dog stand within a twenty-mile radius of their home.

Men know that women know every clean washroom in every mall within a fifty-mile radius of their home.

Men know how to rank hot-dog stands the way women rank public washrooms.

Men know exactly how long it takes to get from the sofa to the refrigerator.

Men know their exact shoe size, whereas women have a vague idea of the general range within two sizes.

Men know that a wallet is supposed to last at least three times as long as the plastic inserts used to hold pictures.

Men know that their wives go through their wallets looking for "things."

Men know that paying five dollars to have a gift wrapped is a waste of four dollars.

Men know that throwing the Sunday funnies away is a waste of good gift-wrapping paper.

Men know that leftover microwave popcorn, pizza, Kraft Macaroni and Cheese and a beer make for a well-balanced breakfast.

Men know what it's like to be the last person to be picked for a game of baseball.

Men know that they have too much body hair.

Men know how to leave just enough paper on a roll of toilet paper to avoid being accused of using the last of the roll.

Men know how to change the toilet paper, but to do so would ruin the game.

Men know that they should never kiss their sister-in-law on the lips.

Men know exactly how much their wives paid for every garment in their closet.

Men know when it's been so long since they bought a new pair of shoes that they will suffer a severe case of sticker shock the next time they do.

Men know how to undo a bra strap.

Men know that it looks bad, but tastes good.

Men know that divorce is like a roller-coaster ride. You can't get off until the ride is over.

Men know that if they don't fart, they will eventually explode.

Men know whose turn it is to buy the next round.

Men know that there's nothing more unattractive than a woman trying to act like a man.

Men know how to avoid paying the check.

Men know that there's a big difference between being in lust and being in love.

Men know exactly how long it takes.

Men know that it's more useful to know where the skeletons are hidden than where the bodies are buried.

Men know that candy is dandy, but liquor is quicker.

Men know if a woman has no self-control.

Men know who's in charge.

Men know that if she's willing, she'll eventually get around to letting you know.

Men know not to take the first cab in line.

Men know how to read a train schedule.

Men know never to order shellfish in a strange restaurant.

Men know that there's nothing as good as an ice cold beer on a hot summer day.

Men know the rules of baseball.

Men know how to fill out a score sheet at a ball game.

Men know that you should do the hard things first.

Men know that you should work hard and play harder.

Men know that sometimes everyone needs to be alone.

Men know that it is possible to put on your pants both legs at the same time.

Men know that women who smoke cigars look stupid.

Men know that there is no such thing as enough.

Men know that a man and a woman can never be just friends.

Men know that women think they know what men know. (Ha!)

Men know that they have no idea what women know and, if they think about it, they don't want to know.

Everything I want is either illegal, immoral, or fattening.

Alexander Woolcott

Men know that you cannot sneak up on a
blind man.

Men know that the best time to take out the
garbage is just before it starts to stink up
the house.

Men know that cutting the grass will not keep it
from growing.

Men know that women don't belong on a
golf course.

Men know that the perfect woman will be able to
throw a ball without looking like she's about
to fall down.

Men know to watch where they step in the barnyard.

Men know that you can't eat the fish until they're cleaned.

Men know that we each have a finite number of heartbeats, and it's better to use them up having sex than working out.

Men know when the shit's too deep to shovel.

Men know when someone thinks their shit doesn't stink.

Men know how to avoid work.

Men know that French food is sissy food.

Men know that a drunk woman is an ugly woman.

Men know that it's all right to cross on the red light as long as you're willing to live with the consequences.

Men know that you have to pay attention to what your children aren't saying.

Men know that eventually you're going to have to trust your kid with the keys to the car.

Men know when to ask their children the hard questions.

Men know that the time to tell your children the facts of life is before they need to know.

Men know how to spot the Eddie Haskells among their children's friends.

Men know if it's too late.

Men know how to scratch an itch.

Men know that your high school reunion is not going to live up to your expectations.

Men know who's yellow.

Men know what fear smells like.

Men know that in the long run, things never even out.

Men know never to sign anything before it's been read by you and your lawyer.

Men know never to let their children read their will.

Men know not to name their ex-wife as the trustee of their children's inheritance.

Men know never to tell their ex-wife anything — never, ever.

Men know better than to give their children everything.

Men know that children need well-defined rules by which to live.

Men know that children need to believe in them.

Men know never to play where they collect their pay.

Men know when their children are disappointed in them.

Men know what a great place Disney World is to visit.

Men know that there are no new ideas, only concepts restated.

Men know how to calculate a 15% tip without taking off their shoes.

Men know that you may date a tramp, but you never bring one home to meet your mother.

Men know that around forty, the bloom begins to go off the rose.

Men know when they're about to be dumped.

Men know that right turns are not always permitted.

Men know which women are not approachable.

Men know where to meet women.

Men know that women can't resist a sad story.

Men know that women find dangerous men exciting.

Men know that most women do not like to be teased.

Men know when it's been good for a woman.

Men know how to fish.

Men know that golf is the only game that doesn't require an umpire.

Men know that the penalty for cheating on your wife can be worse than death.

Men know when it's time to tell your boss to take the job and shove it.

Men know when to swear and when not to swear.

Men know a bitch when they see one.

Men know how to make a task last longer than necessary.

Men know that sometimes it's necessary to work off the clock.

Men know when their boss expects some extra effort in order to get the job done.

Men know that no one really wants to walk the dog.

Men know that no one really wants to empty the cat litter.

Men know that cats are evil and cannot be trusted.

Men know how to bury their kid's dead pets.

Men know that cow pies are not sold at
Baker's Square.

Men know where to hide.

Men know when a woman is telling the truth.

Men know where women like to hide things they
don't want their husbands to see.

Men know if it's going to hurt.

Men know when their children are in trouble.

Men know when a woman has a sense of humor.

Men know which women will appreciate a good
dirty joke.

Men know that you can only protect your kids from the world for so long, then you have to let them bleed a little.

Men know that if they don't check on their kid's pet sooner or later, it will die from neglect.

Men know that watching a cat throw up a hair ball is a pretty disgusting sight.

Men know that you can't keep a woman around if she wants to go.

Men know that it's not fair to blame your wife for your mother's mistakes.

Men know that it's a lot safer to let a woman win an argument.

Men know that trying to win an argument with a woman is like trying to win the Lotto — the odds are 12 million to one.

Men know when their ties are no longer fashionable.

Men know that going shopping with a woman is a trip to boredom.

Men know that hell is a mall.

Men know that the only place they can sing is in the shower.

Men know that their children believe they don't have a clue.

Men know that Rap is crap.

Men know that some women look good naked
and many more do not.

Men know that a woman is going to do exactly
what she wants to do, come hell or
high water.

Men know that most women prefer to make love
in the dark.

Men know never to trust a woman who kisses
with her eyes open. Just what the hell is she
looking at?

Men know where to touch a woman.

Men know that all men are alike, no matter what
they profess to be.

Men know that no matter what the reason may be, never to go into the women's room.

Men know that breast feeding is not attractive.

Men know that once you have a child, the sex is never the same.

Men know how much things should cost.

Men know how to read an annual report.

Men know that the stock market is a very dangerous playing field.

Men know never to invest in futures; it's a sucker's game.

**Blondes have more fun
because they are easier to find
in the dark.**

Unknown

Men know more dirty jokes than the cleaner variety.

Men know that it's a lot cheaper to put new soles and heels on a pair of shoes than to buy a new pair.

Men know that you should clean a pair of suit pants twice as often as you clean the jacket.

Men know that a laundered shirt with light starch makes a better impression than a wash-and-wear shirt.

Men know that you can waste a lot of time planning to do something.

Men know that you can only hold in your stomach for so long before you begin to cramp up.

Men know that women smell good, at least most of the time.

Men know that when it's OK to flirt with a married woman, she'll let you know.

Men know a PT every time.

Men know that some of the ugliest women make the best wives.

Men know when another man is not so manly.

Men know when a woman is after a husband.

Men know when to run and when to fight.

Men know that when a woman makes up her mind, it's only a temporary condition.

Men know that their long-term memory sucks, and their short-term memory isn't much better.

Men know that a woman cuts hair a lot better than a man.

Men know that cooking is not as bad as they would have women believe.

Men know that mowing the grass is a great way to get away from it all.

Men know that the Three Stooges represent classic entertainment.

Men know when it's time to cut bait and when it's time to fish.

Men know to avoid women who's favorite breakfast meal is biscuits and gravy.

Men know that there are some things one must never tell to a woman.

Men know how to drink beer from a bottle.

Men know how to manage. Women know how to micro-manage.

Men know that it's OK to piss in the woods; Mother Nature can take a joke.

Men know about how long it takes.

Men know that it's easier to buy a $300,000 house than it is to buy a $20,000 car.

Men know that it's cool to own a red sports car.

Men know what's cool and what ain't.

Men know when something's way cool and when something sucks the big one.

Men know that you can't give a woman your love without first giving her your soul.

Men know at what temperature beer tastes the best.

Men know that no tie is worth more than fifteen bucks.

Men know to always keep the receipt when giving a woman a gift; she's going to want to return it for some reason.

Men know that Ron Santo was one of the three best third basemen that ever played the game.

Men know that it doesn't get any better than the first time.

Men know that she's not going to tell you everything.

Men know who shot the sheriff.

Men know that a woman will take what she
wants long before you are ready to give it
to her.

Men know how to out wait their enemies.

Men know who can be counted on to show up.

Men know that a job is just a job.

Men know that your work should be something
that you love to do.

Men know that eventually we all lose our hair.

Men know how to make a woman blush.

Men know that you drive for show and putt for dough.

Men know when it's too wet to plow.

Men know never to call a woman's father a piss ass liar.

Men know when someone has a brass pair.

Men know when to come and when to go.

Men know shit from shinola.

Men know when the horse has left the barn.

Men know that a boss is just a person with a lot more to say.

Men know that the fastest way to clear a room is with a fart.

Men know how come.

Men know why children ask so many questions. It's because the little bastards know how dumb their parents really are.

Men know how to use a level and a plumb bob.

Men know how to clean the wax from their ears with the eraser on the end of a pencil.

Men know 3,184 different ways to describe the act of sexual intercourse.

Men know that Tutuphobia, the fear that your son will become a ballet dancer, is a common disorder.

Men know women don't understand a
man's fascination with guns, cars and
naked women.

Men know that most women believe that
baseball is a boring game where loudmouthed
men drink too much beer.

Men know that there are no saints in the
locker room.

Men know no woman is worth your spending
two hours at a Barry Manilow concert.

Men know it's impossible to extract an apology
from your wife.

Men know there are no winners in the game of
life, only survivors and casualties.

Men know shit flows down.

Men know money is as good as any method for keeping score.

Men know never to spit in the umpire's face.

Men know that as you travel the road of life, it's not a good idea to burn too many bridges.

Men know that there are not enough weekends in the year.

Men know not every question deserves an honest, well thought-out answer. A simple lie can save a lot of time.

Men know Henry VIII had a well-executed plan.

Men know not all dogs have their day.

Men know that in every large Catholic family there are two kinds of people: the quick and the hungry.

Men know that to refer to a woman as a schmuck may be appropriate even if it's anatomically incorrect.

Men know "going commando" may be a risky fashion statement.

Men know few women look quite as appealing the morning after as they did the night before.

Men know the good, the bad, and the ugly are not mutually exclusive.

Men know the clinically insane and the truly boring do not have a well-developed sense of humor.

Men know there is always a right way and a wrong way, and most women will take credit for having discovered the former.

Men know that the longer you know an easy woman, the harder it becomes to remember why you found her so interesting.

Men know never to plan a surprise party for your wife's 40th birthday; a wake is much more appropriate.

Men know never to suggest that their wife's first husband is a lucky SOB.

Men are superior to women.
For one thing, they can urinate
from a speeding car.

Will Durst

Men know that trying to fill an inside straight is a sucker bet.

Men know that in the event of marital strife, you should get to the safety deposit box as quickly as possible.

Men know to file first and ask for custody of the children.

Men know never to tell your wife anything that you wouldn't tell your mother or your priest.

Men know rock and roll can save your mortal soul.

Men know Madonna is not.

Men know if you're going to call a woman a bitch, you should be prepared to duck.

Men know time and gravity are woman's mortal enemies.

Men know never to ask a woman her age, weight or the time on her biological clock.

Men know the term "slut" is never used as a proper noun.

Men know it's never too late to say no or to walk away from an ugly woman.

Men know there's always time for one more.

Men know that many a man has gone out for a pack of cigarettes and never returned. Must be the nicotine.

Men know a divorce is never truly over until your ex is dead and buried.

Men know life was about as good as it was going to get the day you were born.

Men know that when given the choice between having a meaningful conversation with a beautiful woman for an hour or seeing her naked for thirty seconds, a man will choose the thirty seconds of nudity every time.

Men know that a woman who cannot see her feet is either pregnant or the victim of too many Big Mac attacks.

Men know that the more cats a woman owns, the less likely she is to be married.

Men know that men are fully capable of understanding the opposite sex; they're just not that interested in any endeavor that does not involve sports or sex.

Men know that asking a woman if she'd like to shack up for the night is like asking her if she'd like her eyes poked out with a darning needle. The answer is seldom yes.

Men know that after the sixth date, a woman begins to hum the wedding march in her sleep.

Men know there are no good answers to the question "If I died, how soon would you remarry?"

Men know never to tell a woman your ATM PIN number.

Men know never to marry a woman whose father demands a camel and two goats as a dowry.

Men know never to give a woman the access code to your answering machine.

Men know a woman would rather die than tell a man that she loves him before he tells her.

Men know there is no good way to tell a woman that she has surpassed her fighting weight.

Men know that time does not heal all wounds.

Men know we all have a finite number of heartbeats, and as few as possible should be wasted on exercise.

Men know when women and fruit are ripe for the picking.

Men know in order to win an argument with a woman, you have to be willing to forgo physical contact with her until you are willing to admit that you may have been wrong.

Men know if it weren't for sex, women wouldn't get their way as often as they do.

Men know never to tell a woman that she can have anything she wants if she'll just stop crying.

Men know never to run away from a fight that you know you can win.

Men know to avoid the temptation to ask a woman to rub your feet.

Men know to always give a woman two gifts on any occasion: an expensive one and a sentimental one.

Men know plaid shirts and a striped tie make a strong fashion statement; so does wearing your wife's underwear.

Men know that because most glue is made from animal parts, licking a stamp is like licking a dead horse.

Men know not to argue with the windows open or while your wife has a carving knife in her hands.

Men know never to take sides when your wife and her mother are arguing, or you'll end up with the blame in every case.

Men know that no matter the task, the tools a
man brings to the job are adequate.

Men know that there are two ways to accomplish
any task: the truly elegant way and the butt
ass ugly way.

Men know that no one ever remembers who won
the silver medal.

Men know that there are at least three sides to
every story: yours, hers and the truth.

Men know that time is on no one's side.

Men know that you're old when you would
rather take a nap then have sex.

Men know that you're really old when your
children begin to call you "the Drooler."

Men know that if she looks like your mother, run.

Men know that a singles bar is not the best place to meet the future mother of your children.

Men know that nothing is more pathetic than a woman who won't dress her age.

Men know that things are seldom equal.

Men know that if you can't sing, don't join the choir.

Men know that you can pick your friends and you can pick your nose, but you can't eat your friends.

Men know that given a choice, a woman will choose a man with hair.

Men know that a cheap cigar is the best repellent for mosquitoes, women and children.

Men know that if a woman tells you she's late, ask her for what before you piss in your pants.

Men know that Mother Nature's most effective aphrodisiac is still a naked woman.

Men know that you can't please everyone, so you've got to please yourself.

Men know that you should never hint that a woman's nose, ears or feet are too big.

Men know that PMS is Mother Nature's way of telling you to get out of the house.

Men know that after about the third face lift, most women begin to look like a well-preserved cadaver.

Men know that if you're stupid enough to piss into the wind, you deserve every drop.

Men know that there may be sex after sixty, but let's hope it's in the dark.

Men know that for every woman who fakes an orgasm, there is a man who could care less.

Men know that an extended visit from your in-laws can do more to harm your marriage than an occasional fling.

Men know that after about a year of marriage, your yin is always wrong and her yang is always right.

Men know that a woman with a tattoo will do just about anything.

Men know that Anna Nicole Smith will never drown.

Men know to never attempt to end an argument with the phrase "Whatever you say dear" or "Blow it out your ass."

Men know to beware of any woman who refers to your offspring as "her children."

Men know to never shake hands in the restroom.

Men know to measure twice and cut once.

Men know to beware of any man who tells you that his favorite number is 69.

Never date a woman you can hear ticking.

Mark Patinkin

Men know to avoid women who smoke cigars and spit.

Men know that after 40, women should not wear skirts if the hem is above their knees. It's not as attractive as Liz Claiborne would have them believe.

Men know never to let anyone give your son a Barbie doll.

Men know never to tell your in-laws that you have pictures of their daughter in the buff.

Men know that men can bond over something as simple as a fart or a belch.

Men know that women do not appreciate the cinematic excellence of the campfire scene in *Blazing Saddles.*

Men know that a great date always ends with sex and a hearty "Hi-Ho Silver, can I call you a cab?"

Men know that there is very little difference between a wedding and a funeral. The major participants never live happily ever after.

Men know that death is Mother Nature's way of telling you just who's in charge.

Men know that the more cats a man has, the less likely it is that he is married and the more likely it is that he lives with his mother.

Men know that the normal affection that a man should feel for his mother lies somewhere between that of Oedipus and Norman Bates.

Men know to avoid any woman whose nickname is Easy Rider.

Men know that the amount of cleavage a single woman is willing to show is directly proportionate to how fast her biological clock is ticking.

Men know to avoid any blind date described as a "two bagger."

Men know never to ask a woman if she'd like a cooking lesson from your mother.

Men know that the Bill of Rights does not apply to children, husbands and anyone stupid enough to believe anything their divorce lawyer tells them.

Men know that anyone who will chew tobacco will eat shit.

Men know that if Wilt Chamberlain screwed as many women as he claims, his dick would be worn down to a stub.

Men know to avoid men who hang around
petting zoos.

Men know when a woman refers to an oxymoron
she's talking about a sensitive man.

Men know when a man refers to an oxymoron
he's talking about feminine instincts.

Men know that artificial insemination is the
ultimate cut-off.

Men know that if a woman wants to put the
magic back into a relationship, she should
consider doing a few tricks herself.

Men know that what looks bad often
tastes good.

Men know that you can give a woman your love,
but she won't be satisfied until you give her
your soul.

Men know that if you want a vacation, send your
    children to summer camp and your wife to
    the fat farm.

Men know to never ask a woman to marry you
    until you've seen her naked in the morning,
    angry and drunk. She will never be
    less attractive.

Men know that no woman ever gave a man full
    credit for his participation in the
    reproductive process.

Men know that if we could dance like Fred
    Astaire, we wouldn't be interested in
    dancing with women.

Men know that a "nooner" has nothing to do
    with lunch in the traditional sense.

Men know that when a woman orders a Big Mac,
    large fries and a Diet Coke, she's only
    fooling herself.

Men know that where a man will shout, a woman will throw.

Men know that a marriage is in trouble when a man refers to his wife as the former woman of his dreams.

Men know that a marriage is in trouble when a woman begins to refer to her husband as the alleged father of her children.

Men know that a marriage is in trouble when the children begin to refer to their father as their dad, the respondent.

Men know that love is being able to take a shower with a woman without turning off the lights.

Men know to avoid women who dress and undress in the closet.

When confronted with two
evils, a man will always choose
the prettier.

Unknown

Men know that if you're going to kiss another man's wife, be sure to keep your tongue to yourself.

Men know that just about the time you think you've got it licked, someone changes the rules.

Men know that if a woman requires more maintenance than your car, it may be time to trade her in on a newer model.

Men know women with long fingernails should not be allowed to handle heavy machinery or any other manly piece of equipment.

Men know that any woman who accepts a blind date is about five times more desperate than a man.

Men know that if a man had been meant to change diapers, he would have been born without the sense of smell.

Men know that if women were as loyal and friendly as a dog, there would be far fewer divorces in the world.

Men know that if a woman would lick you every time you came home, there would be no reason to own a dog.

Men know that losing a woman is like losing a wisdom tooth, it may hurt at first but after a while, you don't even know it's not there.

Men know that any woman who drinks like a man and swears like a man should be treated like a man.

Men know that a drunken woman is like a drunken man, except that she's not nearly as amusing or attractive.

Men know that watching most women throw a ball is like watching a man dance *Swan Lake*: unattractive and unappealing.

Men know that they should never admit to their priest that Judas was their favorite apostle.

Men know that for some reason, a woman's biological clock prevents her from being anywhere on time.

Men know that when a woman tells you she's a vegetarian, it doesn't necessarily rule out certain forms of sexual activity.

Men know that a woman with a list of goals and a determined look on her face will scare the hell out of most men.

Men know that after the first child, women begin to wear their shirts untucked in order to conceal their hips.

Men know that in the entire history of the human race, no man has ever heard a woman fart.

Men know that when a woman tells you that she'd like to knead your dough, she may also be willing to frost your cookies.

Men know that there is nothing more attractive than a woman who has said yes to every question you have asked her.

Men know that it appears that women drive cars the same way they make love, with their eyes closed.

Men know that all of the pleasure went out of flying when the airlines let older women and their sons become flight attendants.

Men know that a man's worse nightmare is a blind date with a woman who looks like Tammy Faye Baker and has a voice like Carol Channing.

Men know that if your best friends refer to you as "that bed wetting, draft dodging, commie bastard," you may want to consider a career outside of politics.

Men know that if people tell you that you look like Dom DeLuise, it may be time for a visit to Jenny Craig.

Men know that marriage is the last place to look for happiness and sexual satisfaction.

Men know that when a man meets a woman for the first time, the first thing that goes through his mind is "Would I kick her out of bed for eating crackers?"

Men know that when a woman meets a man for the first time, the question she asks herself is "How much does this guy make per year?"

Men know that at any gathering, every man in the room knows exactly where the best-looking woman is at any time.

Men know that some little known and appreciated force of nature drives men towards cleavage and short skirts.

Men know that a mini skirt was God's gift to women with great legs and a curse to the other 99.9% of the female population.

Men know that the oldest profession is prostitution because every woman since the dawn of time demands something before she'll give it up.

Men know that when a woman tells you that she needs you, she probably wants you to lift or carry something.

Men know that men have been mentored from
an early age to get as much as they can.

Men know that no man ever respected a woman
the morning after, or any time in the near
or distant future.

Men know that it's a whole lot easier to tell a
naked woman that you love her than one
who is fully clothed. In either case, you may
not mean it, but it seems easier with her
bare skin pressed against yours.

Men know to beware of a woman whose "G" spot
is located in your bank account.

Men know that everyone should make love in the
back seat of a car at least once in their life.

Men know that there's nothing more annoying than a woman with money, unless it's a woman with your money.

Men know that if a woman isn't buying something, she feels a lack of purpose.

Men know that a good-looking woman with a brain is a waste of one or the other.

Men know that no feminist was ever married to a happy man.

Men know that a perfect woman is physically fit, attractive and not too bright.

Men know to treat women like a good set of car tires: rotate them every six thousand miles.

Men know that the only games that matter are the ones that include a stick or a ball.

Men know that if you're not playing basketball, you shouldn't be dribbling.

Men know that before you marry a divorced woman, you should have a drink with her former husband.

Men know that when a woman tells a man her innermost thoughts, she might as well be making a long distance call to the land of I Don't Give A Rat's Ass.

Men know that if you want to go where no man has gone before, try explaining the infield fly rule to a woman.

Men know that if your best friend tells you that he'd like to get in touch with your feminine side, run like the wind.

Men know that death and Alzheimer's are the only acceptable excuses for forgetting a woman's birthday or your wedding anniversary.

Wicked women bother me. Good women bore me. That is the only difference between them.

Oscar Wilde

Men know that imitation and a hard-on are often the sincerest forms of flattery.

Men know that you may need to get a life if your social calendar and the *TV Guide* are one and the same.

Men know that there is nothing like a dame.

Men know that there is much about the female amatory that should forever remain a mystery.

Men know that the Wonderbra should be a staple in every woman's wardrobe.

Men know that the entire male population breathed a sigh of relief when women stopped wearing girdles and when they began wearing bras with hooks in the front.

Men know that the last things we want to know are when a woman is retaining water and when her period is particularly heavy.

Men know that one of man's greatest achievements is surviving the Age of Reason with his sense of humor still intact.

Men know that had God wanted men to be politically correct, He would have created them without a penis, devoid of a sense of humor and spineless — pretty much every woman's dream date.

Men know that younger men marry older women because their own mothers are not available.

Men know that younger women marry older men because they can.

Men know that men going through a midlife crisis will search out younger women to scratch their seven-year itch.

Men know that men look back on a life full of fond memories, while women look back on a life full of regrets.

Men know women make great politicians because they have experience faking it.

Men know that if the glass ceiling were a mirror, most women would stop complaining.

Men know that if childbirth were such a wonderful experience, women would not be screaming and begging for drugs during the process.

Men know Shakespeare was wrong; the world is not a stage, it's an elevator.

Men know that if a woman wants a man to love her, she had better treat him like the supreme being that he is.

Men know the perfect date is a woman who shows up with a pizza and a six pack.

Men know that it's been too long since you've had sex if you can't find the keys to your handcuffs.

Men know that you're in love if you believe that one woman differs from another.

Men know the perfect marriage involves a blind man and a mute woman.

Men know that a wife is what's left after the sex has gone out of the marriage.

Men know sex is like having money in a savings account; you should leave it in only as long as there's interest.

Men know that the first half of life is ruined by your parents and the second by your wives.

Men know that moral victories don't count.

Men know that the sex drive begins at puberty and ends at marriage.

Men know that any woman worth having is worth lying and cheating to get.

Men know that any woman worth having is worth lying and cheating to keep.

Men know that men are superior because they
can pee without dropping their shorts.

Men know that more men's lives have been
ruined by women than by liquor.

Men know the only good thing that came out of
the women's movement was the rebirth of
the Dutch Treat date.

Men know that some women rely on their looks
as a means of birth control.

Men know an inexperienced woman is one
who believes that fellatio is Pinnochio's
twin brother.

Men know that kinky sex involves a feather
duster and that perverted sex involves a
vacuum cleaner.

Men know a virgin is a woman who believes that mutual orgasm is an investment strategy.

Men know that you need a haircut if you begin to look like Don King.

Men know that the game of life has no overtime.

Men know the game of life should be played in sudden death mode.

Men know that the easiest way to get noticed is to die young.

Men know that you don't have to take your clothes off for sex to be fun.

Men know sex is not a team sport.

As a guy, you're raised to get as much as you can.

Woody Harrelson

Men know that divorce creates more unwed
mothers than premarital sex.

Men know that some women only become
interesting after you've had a few drinks.

Men know there is nothing happier than a
schizophrenic woman; she always has
someone to talk to.

Men know that a gentleman is someone who can
belch the national anthem, but doesn't.

Men know that it's dangerous to be right when
your wife is wrong.

Men know that no man can think clearly with
an erection.

Men know never to shake hands with a urologist, proctologist or gynecologist.

Men know that the fact that women have more cookbooks than sex books should tell you something.

Men know that they should behave like men: selfish and childish.

Men know that love is the only game that is not called on account of darkness.

Men know that children may love their parents, but they will never forgive them.

Men know if you can't marry a horny woman, at least marry one who can cook.

Men know that no man ever got past second
base by being politically correct.

Men know there's nothing worse than a PT who
expects a man to be PC.

Men know never to date a woman who asks you
to meet her at her favorite bar.

Men know never to suggest to a woman that you
meet at Hooters.

Woman is made for man. Man is made for life.

Richard Burton

Send check or money order for $19.99 plus
$5.00 S&H (Sorry, no CODs) to:

MAPs
1310 Waukegan Road, Suite 320
Glenview, IL 60025

Name: _____

Address: _____

City: _____ **State:** _____ **Zip:** _____

Telephone: _____

Name to be printed on certificate:

_____

Men Are Pigs Society
Join Today!

Whether it's for you, or for the pig in your life, a charter membership in The Men Are Pigs Society makes a great gift.

Membership includes:
◆ our exclusive member's baseball cap with our motto, Carpe Diem, and the male symbol embroidered on the front and Men Are Pigs on the back of the cap
◆ a membership certificate suitable for framing
◆ a colorful bumper sticker

Certificate Of Membership

John Doe

Is a Charter Member in

The Men Are Pigs Society

In the event that you would like to share your favorite bits of masculine knowledge, I'd like to offer you the opportunity to submit as many nuggets of wisdom that come to mind. If I like something that you submit, and it meets our high standards of good taste, it may be included in Men Are Pigs II.

Please send your contributions to:

MAPS
1310 Waukegan Road, Suite 320
Glenview, IL 60025

Or e-mail your contributions to:

menarepigs@aol.com